J 359.9606 MIL AR 6.1 PTS 1
Miller, Adam
U. S. Marines true stories:
Tales of bravery

EDGE
BOOKS™

COURAGE
UNDER FIRE

U.S. MARINES TRUE STORIES

TALES OF BRAVERY

BY ADAM MILLER

CAPSTONE PRESS
a capstone imprint

Edge Books are published by Capstone Press,
1710 Roe Crest Drive, North Mankato, Minnesota 56003
www.capstonepub.com

Library of Congress Cataloging-in-Publication Data
Miller, Adam, 1970–
  U.S. Marines true stories : tales of bravery / by Adam Miller.
     pages cm—(Edge books. Courage under fire)
  Audience: Ages 8–12.
  Includes bibliographical references and index.
  Summary: "Provides gripping accounts of Marine servicemen and servicewomen who showed
exceptional courage during combat"—Provided by publisher.
  ISBN 978-1-4765-9935-9 (library binding)
  ISBN 978-1-4765-9940-3 (eBook PDF)
1. United States. Marine Corps—Juvenile literature. 2. Marines—United States—Juvenile
literature. 3. Courage—Juvenile literature. I. Title.
  VE23.M528 2015
  359.9′6092273—dc23   2014004281

Editorial Credits
Christopher L. Harbo and Anna Butzer, editors; Veronica Scott, designer; Gene Bentdahl,
production specialist

Photo Credits
Corbis: ACME, 9, 11; Getty Images: Keystone, 8, Scott Peterson, 26; iStockphotos: lauradyoung, 5
(SS), 19 (SS); NARA: U.S. Marine Corps, 14, U.S. Marine Corps/SSgt. W.W. Frank, 12, U.S. Navy,
18; Newscom: Everett Collection, 6; Shutterstock: Jim Barber, 5 (DSC), R Carner, 5 (BS, PH); U.S.
Marine Corps photo, 21, 22, 24, 28, Cpl. Andres J. Lugo, 15, Cpl. Brian J. Slaght, cover (inset), Cpl.
Randall A. Clinton, 20, Cpl. Reece Lodder, cover, 3, Gunnery Sgt. Kevin W. Williams, 29, Lance Cpl.
Christofer P. Baines, 17, Sgt. Jeffery Cordero, 16, Sgt. Luis R. Agostini, 27, Staff Sgt. Ryan Smith, 25;
Wikipedia: DoD photo, 5 (LOM, MOH, NC, NMCCM) 9 (MOH), 13, (MOH), 17 (NC)

Design Elements
Shutterstock: Filipchuk Oleg Vasiliovich, locote, Oleg Zabielin, Petr Vaclavek

Direct Quotations:
Page 7 from *George W. Hamilton, USMC: America's Greatest World War I Hero* by Mark Mortensen
     (Jefferson, N.C.: McFarland & Company, 2011).
Page 10 from "Colonel Peter Julien Ortiz: OSS Marine, Actor, Californian" by Benis Frank (California
     State Military Museum, www.militarymuseum.org/Ortiz.html).
Page 13 from Marine Corps Decade Timeline (www.marines.com/history-heritage/timeline).
Page 16 from "Decades Later, Marine Awarded for Heroism in Vietnam" by Jeffery Cordero (9th
     Marine Corps District, www.9thmcd.marines.mil/News/NewsArticleDisplay/tabid/4722/
     Article/142522/decades-later-marine-awarded-for-heroism-in-vietnam.aspx).
Page 17 from "Marine Receives Navy Cross for Actions in Vietnam War" by Christofer P. Baines
     (U.S. Department of Defense, www.defense.gov/News/NewsArticle. aspx?ID=62788).
Page 19 from "Persian Gulf War Hero Shares Silver Star with Pilot Killed in Vietnam—His Dad
     Ceremony: Pennsylvanian was 2 Months Old When Father Went Off to War" Deseret News, July
     3, 1991 (www.deseretnews.com/article/170774/PERSIAN-GULF-WAR-HERO-SHARES-SILVER-
     STAR-WITH-PILOT-KILLED-IN--VIETNAM--HIS-DAD-CEREMONY.html?pg=all).
Pages 22 and 24 from "Remarks by the President Awarding the Medal of Honor to Sergeant Dakota
     Meyer" by President Barack Obama (www.whitehouse.gov/the-press-office/2011/09/15/remarks-
     president-awarding-medal-honor-sergeant-dakota-meyer).

Printed in the United States of America in Stevens Point, Wisconsin
032014   008092WZF14

TABLE OF CONTENTS

ALWAYS FAITHFUL

The Marine Corps traces its roots back more than 200 years. This branch of the U.S. military got its start on November 10, 1775. At that time it was called the Continental Marines. During the Revolutionary War (1775–1783), the Continental Marines fought on both land and sea. They were often the first soldiers to face the enemy in battle.

When the Revolutionary War ended, the United States no longer needed as much protection. The Continental Marines **disbanded**. But as the United States quickly grew, so did the threats to the new nation. In 1798 President John Adams brought the Marine Corps back to help the Navy. Ever since, the Marines have fought in every major U.S. war. Though a separate branch, it remains under Navy command to this day.

The Marine Corps' **motto**, Semper Fidelis, is Latin for "Always Faithful." No matter where duty takes them, Marines hold this motto close to their hearts. They are faithful to their fellow soldiers, their country, and their fight for freedom. In the stories that follow, you'll witness the faithfulness of many Marines who showed remarkable courage under fire.

disband—to remove a military unit from active service
motto—a short statement that tells what a person or organization believes in or stands for

MILITARY AWARDS

Medal of Honor:
the highest award
for bravery in the
U.S. military

**Distinguished
Service Cross:**
the second-highest
military award for
bravery that is given
to members of the
U.S. Army (and Air Force
prior to 1960)

Navy Cross:
the second-highest
military award for
bravery that is given
to members of the
Navy and Marines

Silver Star:
the third-highest
award for bravery in
the U.S. military

Bronze Star:
the fourth-highest
award for bravery in
the U.S. military

Legion of Merit:
the sixth-highest
award for bravery in
the U.S. military

Purple Heart:
an award given to
members of the military
wounded by the enemy
in combat

**Navy and Marine Corps
Commendation Medal:**
an award given to
members of the
Navy and Marines
for sustained acts
of heroism and
meritorious service

WORLD WAR I

DATES: 1914–1918

THE COMBATANTS: ALLIES (MAIN
COUNTRIES: GREAT BRITAIN, FRANCE,
ITALY, RUSSIA, UNITED STATES) VS.
CENTRAL POWERS (MAIN COUNTRIES:
GERMANY, AUSTRIA-HUNGARY, BULGARIA,
OTTOMAN EMPIRE)

THE VICTOR: ALLIES

CASUALTIES: ALLIES—5,142,631 DEAD;
CENTRAL POWERS—3,386,200 DEAD

Marines clash with the Germans in the Battle of
Belleau Wood during World War I.

CAPTAIN GEORGE HAMILTON

On June 6, 1918, Captain George Hamilton led his Marines in the Battle of Belleau Wood. This battle in the wooded hills of France was one of the bloodiest of World War I. Using darkness for cover, Hamilton's mission was to clear the Germans from a hilltop 800 yards (732 meters) away.

At 3:45 a.m. Hamilton and his troops advanced on the German line. Almost immediately they faced heavy machine gun fire. "We hadn't moved 50 yards when [the Germans] cut loose at us from the woods ahead," Hamilton later recalled. "[It was] more machine guns then I had ever heard before."

Pinned to the ground, Hamilton crawled on his belly. He encouraged any able Marines to follow him as he weaved in and out of the woods. Then they darted across a field and entered another wooded area. As enemy fire rained down, Hamilton and his men rushed over the hill. He used his **bayonet** to bring down German soldiers blocking his path. The hole he created in the German line allowed more Marines to rush in. By the end of the day, they had taken control of the hill. For his courage Hamilton earned the Navy Cross and two Distinguished Service Crosses.

bayonet—a long metal blade attached to the end of a musket or rifle

WORLD WAR II

Dates: 1939–1945

The Combatants: Allies (main countries: Great Britain, France, Russia, United States) vs. Axis Powers (main countries: Germany, Italy, Japan)

The Victor: Allies

Casualties: Allies—14,141,544 dead; Axis—5,634,232 dead

Marines battle a fire in an aircraft hangar at Henderson Field on the island of Guadalcanal in November 1942.

GUNNERY SERGEANT JOHN BASILONE

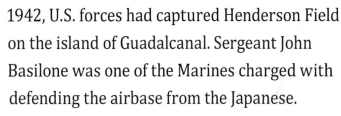

During World War II, the United States battled the Japanese in the Pacific Ocean. By late 1942, U.S. forces had captured Henderson Field on the island of Guadalcanal. Sergeant John Basilone was one of the Marines charged with defending the airbase from the Japanese.

On October 24 about 3,000 Japanese soldiers attacked Basilone's position. Fighting in rain and mud, Basilone and his 15 men defended their position from two machine gun stations.

Heavily outnumbered, the two-day battle didn't go well for Basilone and his men. When the Japanese took out one of the gun stations, only Basilone and two other Marines remained able to fight. But he didn't give up. Basilone lifted his 100-pound (45-kilogram) machine gun and ran to the empty gun station. From there he hammered away at the endless enemy attacks.

When his ammunition ran low, Basilone armed himself with a pistol. He dashed for a supply area now behind enemy lines. He grabbed all the ammo he could carry and raced back to the gun station. After fighting through a second night, the Japanese finally withdrew. Basilone and his men had protected Henderson Field. He earned the Medal of Honor for his actions.

COLONEL PETER ORTIZ

Peter Ortiz was born in the United States and moved to France as a child. In 1939 he joined the French Foreign Legion. This branch of the French army allowed foreigners living in France to fight in World War II. In 1940 Ortiz was shot in the leg and captured by the Germans. During 15 months in prison camps, he attempted several escapes. Finally, in October 1941, he was successful and made his way to the United States. Less than a year later, he enlisted in the Marines and headed back to war.

While stationed in North Africa, Ortiz was assigned to the Office of Strategic Services (OSS). He worked with secret agents from England and France. In January 1944 the group parachuted into France. They met up with French Resistance members fighting against the **Nazis** controlling the country.

Ortiz and his men moved often, keeping their location secret. One night Ortiz disguised himself and entered a café in a German-occupied town. He overheard a Nazi comment on "the filthy American swine" that were helping the French Resistance. The comment angered Ortiz. He shed his costume and confronted the Nazis with a pistol in each hand. Guns blazing, Ortiz took out the Nazis and fled the scene.

In August 1944 the Germans spotted Ortiz and other Marines in the small town of Centron. Ortiz and the other Marines bolted. They hid in the homes of friendly French townspeople. But Ortiz knew that if they didn't **surrender**, the Nazis would hurt the residents. After talking to his fellow Marines, they agreed to turn themselves in. They spent the rest of the war in a prison camp, but the townspeople were left unharmed.

After the war Ortiz was released from prison and he returned to the United States. For his bravery during the war he earned two Navy Crosses, the Legion of Merit, and two Purple Hearts.

Peter Ortiz arrives in New York in 1941 after having escaped from a German prison camp.

Nazi—a member of a political party led by Adolf Hitler; the Nazis ruled Germany from 1933 to 1945
surrender—to give up or admit defeat in battle

THE KOREAN WAR

DATES: 1950–1953

THE COMBATANTS: THE UNITED STATES, SOUTH KOREA, AND UNITED NATIONS (UN) TROOPS VS. NORTH KOREA AND CHINA

THE VICTOR: NO VICTOR; THE UN AND NORTH KOREA SIGNED A TRUCE, BUT NO PERMANENT PEACE TREATY WAS EVER SIGNED BY NORTH KOREA AND SOUTH KOREA

CASUALTIES: UNITED STATES, UN, AND SOUTH KOREA—256,631 DEAD; CHINESE AND NORTH KOREANS—ESTIMATED 1,006,000 DEAD

First Lieutenant Baldomero Lopez (top) leads the charge over the seawall in the Battle of Inchon.

FIRST LIEUTENANT BALDOMERO LOPEZ

When the Korean War began, North Korea won some of the early battles. But within a few months, UN forces began pushing back. Win or lose, they knew the Battle of Inchon on September 15, 1950, would be critical. UN forces needed a stronghold near North Korea, and Seoul, the South Korean capital, was close to Inchon. First Lieutenant Baldomero "Punchy" Lopez was part of the risky invasion to eventually retake Seoul.

When Lopez and his **platoon** landed in Inchon, the beach exploded with enemy fire. The wide-open beach left the men totally exposed. Using ladders, Lopez led his men over a towering seawall. With bullets buzzing by, Lopez topped the wall first. Once over, he spotted an enemy bunker. Lopez grabbed a hand grenade and yanked out the pin. As he wound up to throw, bullets tore into his chest and right shoulder. The live grenade tumbled out of his hand.

Severely injured, Lopez crawled toward the grenade. He tried to grasp it but couldn't. He knew he must get the grenade away from his men. With seconds left, he pulled the grenade under his body. The blast killed Lopez instantly, but his sacrifice saved the other Marines. A war reporter later said, "... [Lopez] died with the courage that makes men great." Lopez **posthumously** received the Medal of Honor for his sacrifice.

platoon—a small group of soldiers who work together
posthumous—coming or happening after death

THE VIETNAM WAR

DATES: 1959–1975

THE COMBATANTS: UNITED STATES, SOUTH VIETNAM, AND THEIR ALLIES VS. NORTH VIETNAM AND ITS ALLIES

THE VICTOR: NORTH VIETNAM

CASUALTIES: UNITED STATES–58,220 DEAD; SOUTH VIETNAM–ESTIMATED 200,000 TO 250,000 DEAD; NORTH VIETNAM–ESTIMATED 1.1 MILLION DEAD

Marines fire their weapons during the Vietnam War.

PRIVATE FIRST CLASS ROBERT RIMPSON

On August 18, 1965, **Private** First Class Robert L. Rimpson took part in Operation Starlite. It was the first major battle the United States fought on the ground in Vietnam. It was also a day that changed 19-year-old Rimpson's life forever.

Rimpson and his fellow soldiers had orders to advance on an enemy **trench**. Suddenly intense gunfire began cutting them down. Wounded soldiers dropped all around him. But Rimpson pushed forward. He fired his rifle and grenade launcher into the trench as fast as he could.

Robert Rimpson in 2013

private—a soldier of the lowest rank
trench—a long, deep area dug into the ground with dirt piled up on one side for defense

After clearing the trench line, Rimpson discovered he was wounded. A shard of **shrapnel** had struck near his eye. But Rimpson didn't give up. With blurry vision, he helped more seriously wounded soldiers reach a rescue helicopter. At the same time, he fired grenades at the enemy. His actions allowed more rescue helicopters to land and take off safely.

After the war Rimpson received a Purple Heart for his injuries. In May 2013 he was also awarded the Bronze Star. After the ceremony Rimpson said, "I've never been more proud to be a Marine."

Rimpson holds up his citation for the Bronze Star during the award ceremony in May 2013.

shrapnel—pieces that have broken off something after an explosion

LANCE CORPORAL NED SEATH

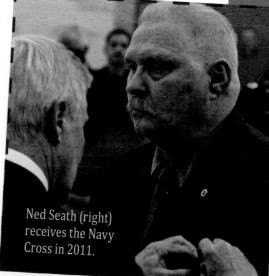

In 1966 Lance Corporal Ned Seath led a machine gun team in Vietnam. Deep in enemy territory, their mission was to block enemy trails running through the jungle.

On July 16 Seath and his men were attacked at night. His key gunner was wounded and a bullet had damaged the soldier's weapon. In total darkness Seath crawled to the injured Marine. He grabbed the broken machine gun and quickly took the weapon apart. Then he did the same with another broken weapon. Suddenly a **mortar** shell exploded nearby. It wounded his hand and leg. But Seath continued putting the pieces of the two weapons together to build one working firearm. Then he stood up, returned fire, and slowed down the attack.

Ned Seath (right) receives the Navy Cross in 2011.

In 2011 Seath received the Navy Cross for his actions that day in Vietnam. At the ceremony Bill Hutton, who fought with Seath, recalled, "If it weren't for Ned Seath, I'd be buried right now ... in Arlington [National Cemetery]. He went above and beyond the call of duty. He saved a company of Marines."

mortar—a short cannon that fires shells or rockets high in the air

OPERATION DESERT STORM

Dates: 1991

The Combatants: United States and coalition forces vs. Iraq

The Victor: United States and coalition forces

Casualties: U.S. and coalition forces—1,065 dead; Iraq—20,000–35,000 dead

An Iraqi tank burns after an attack during Operation Desert Storm.

CORPORAL MICHAEL KILPATRICK

In early 1991, 22-year-old Corporal Michael Kilpatrick experienced two action-packed days while serving during Operation Desert Storm. On February 14, he was driving a support vehicle near Kuwait when it came under heavy mortar fire. Thinking quickly, he managed to speed out of harm's way. Then he called in air strikes to take out the attackers.

The very next day, Kilpatrick spotted two Iraqi tanks and about 40 soldiers in the distance. They were heading toward him and fellow Marine Bryan Zickefoose. Rather than retreat, the two men decided to head off the attack on their **battalion**. Armed with rocket launchers, they charged toward the tanks. As they closed in, each fired a rocket, and they took out both tanks. Then their battalion regrouped and surrounded the Iraqis.

Both Kilpatrick and Zickefoose received Silver Stars for their bravery. Kilpatrick shrugged off his actions. He said, "Somebody saw me doing my job and thought it was special for some reason." Kilpatrick dedicated his award to his father, who died in the Vietnam War in 1969.

battalion—a large group of soldiers

OPERATION ENDURING FREEDOM

DATES: 2001–PRESENT

THE COMBATANTS: AFGHANISTAN GOVERNMENT, THE UNITED STATES AND ITS COALITION FORCES VS. AL-QAIDA **TERRORIST** ORGANIZATION AND THE TALIBAN, AN ISLAMIC GROUP THAT SUPPORTS AL-QAIDA

THE VICTOR: CONFLICT ONGOING

CASUALTIES: AMERICAN AND COALITION FORCES (THROUGH DECEMBER 6, 2012)–3,215 DEAD; AFGHAN CIVILIANS (REPORTED FROM JANUARY 2007 TO JUNE 2012)–13,009 DEAD; TALIBAN AND AL-QAIDA–NUMBER UNKNOWN

U.S. Marines on patrol as they battle Taliban forces in Afghanistan in 2008.

terrorist—a person who uses violence to kill, injure, or make people and governments afraid

FIRST LIEUTENANT REBECCA TURPIN

On December 13, 2008, First Lieutenant Rebecca Turpin led her platoon on a supply mission to Musa Qala, Afghanistan. About seven hours into the mission, an improvised explosive device (IED) hit one of the vehicles in her **convoy**. Turpin ordered a quick search for more IEDs in the area. Two were found and disarmed before the convoy moved on.

Eight hours later Turpin's convoy hit another IED in total darkness. But the group pressed forward until they came to a small village. Suddenly Turpin heard one of her gunners yell, "RPG!" Seconds later a rocket-propelled grenade (RPG) hit their refueling truck's engine. Gunfire and grenades hit and disabled another vehicle. Turpin ordered the convoy to surround the disabled vehicles. Her actions shielded her team as they prepared to tow one vehicle and repair the other. Turpin then called for air support to protect the convoy.

After two and a half days, Turpin's convoy reached Musa Qala with zero casualties. Turpin was awarded the Navy and Marine Corps Commendation Medal for her leadership under enemy fire.

convoy—a group of vehicles traveling together, usually accompanied by armed forces

CORPORAL DAKOTA MEYER

At a ceremony in 2011, President Barack Obama said, "Dakota [Meyer] is the kind of guy who gets the job done." These words reflect the bravery, determination, and quick thinking of Corporal Dakota Meyer during Operation Enduring Freedom.

On September 8, 2009, a morning patrol of American soldiers and Afghan forces walked into the village of Ganjgal, Afghanistan. Before they could meet with people from the village, Taliban fighters ambushed them.

Dakota Meyer and Sergeant Juan Rodriguez-Chavez were stationed about 1 mile (1.6 kilometers) outside of the village. Over the radio they listened to the commands of their fellow soldiers under attack. They knew the patrol was outnumbered and needed help. They radioed a commanding officer for permission to go in. They were told the situation was too dangerous. They asked three more times and were still denied.

Corporal Dakota Meyer stands near the village of Ganjgal in Afghanistan.

Meyer and Rodriguez-Chavez decided they had to act. Meyer said, "Those were my brothers, and I couldn't just sit back and watch." They hopped in a military vehicle and charged into the battle zone. Meyer fired the gun on top of the vehicle and picked up wounded soldiers along the way. When the vehicle was full, they drove to safety and unloaded the wounded. Then they went back in for another load. On the fourth trip, hot shrapnel tore into Meyer's arm. On the fifth, they found a group of four fallen Marines. Through heavy fire, they carried each soldier's body to their vehicle.

Because of their bravery, 23 Afghan allies and 13 Americans survived the attack. Meyer received the Medal of Honor and Rodriguez-Chavez received the Navy Cross for their courage.

Meyer enjoys a quiet moment in the village of Ganjgal, Afghanistan.

SERGEANT RYAN SOTELO

Sergeant Ryan Sotelo served in the 3rd Battalion, 5th Marine Regiment during Operation Enduring Freedom. His unit had more casualties than any other during the conflict. More than 160 of its members had been wounded and 25 were killed in combat.

On November 25, 2010, **insurgents** battered the unit with heavy gunfire. A bullet struck and killed platoon commander 1st Lieutenant William Donnelly almost immediately. Without hesitation, Sotelo took control of the unit. He led troops to a nearby canal for better cover. The unit was safer, but Sotelo didn't stay put for long. He raced back into the gunfire to retrieve his fallen officer.

As he ran Sotelo saw an insurgent firing at his men. He darted toward him while activating a grenade. As he closed in, he tossed the weapon and killed the insurgent. Then he grabbed Donnelly's body and returned to the canal.

As the fighting continued, Sotelo knew they could not win. He slowly withdrew the troops, fighting until they were all safely behind the American line. Sotelo received the Silver Star for his leadership and quick judgment while under fire.

insurgent—a person who rebels and fights against his or her country's ruling government and those supporting it

OPERATION IRAQI FREEDOM

DATES: 2003–2011

THE COMBATANTS: THE UNITED STATES AND COALITION FORCES VS. IRAQ, FIRST THE GOVERNMENT OF SADDAM HUSSEIN AND THEN INSURGENTS

THE VICTOR: THE UNITED STATES DEFEATED SADDAM HUSSEIN IN 2003 BUT THEN FACED STIFF FIGHTING FROM INSURGENTS UNTIL ITS WITHDRAWAL IN 2011

CASUALTIES: AMERICAN AND COALITION FORCES—4,804 DEAD; IRAQI SOLDIERS AND INSURGENTS—ESTIMATED MORE THAN 30,000 DEAD

U.S. Marines clear out houses held by insurgents in Fallujah, Iraq, in 2004.

FIRST SERGEANT BRADLEY KASAL

All Marines believe in the Semper Fi motto. But for some, the promise to be "Always Faithful" shows most in the heat of battle. Such was the case for First Sergeant Bradley Kasal during Operation Iraqi Freedom.

In 2004 Kasal was stationed in Fallujah, Iraq. While helping his platoon, an explosion of gunfire rang from an Iraqi home. Kasal knew that several troops were inside. As soldiers ran from the house, Kasal charged in. While helping a wounded Marine to safety, bullets tore through both of his legs.

Medical supplies ran low quickly. With only enough to bandage one of the wounded Marines, Kasal refused medical treatment.

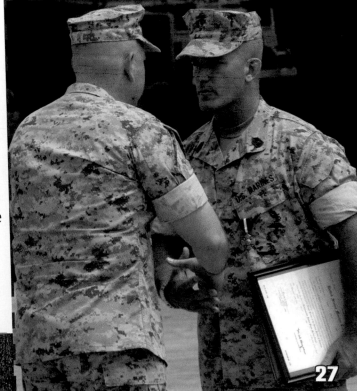

Kasal receives the Navy Cross for his actions in Iraq.

Meanwhile, the insurgents hadn't quit. One tossed a grenade, hoping it would force the Marines to come out of hiding. It rolled within a few feet of the men. Sacrificing his safety, Kasal threw himself between the grenade and the other Marines. His courageous actions saved several of his fellow Marines. When the battle ended, Kasal had been hit by seven rounds of ammo and more than 40 pieces of shrapnel.

Kasal survived his wounds—but just barely. By the time he arrived at a hospital, he had lost 60 percent of his blood. He needed 20 surgeries to save his legs. After recovering, Kasal walked with a limp. But he returned to work as Sergeant Major of the School of Infantry (West) at Camp Pendleton in Southern California. He earned a Navy Cross and a Purple Heart for his actions in Iraq.

Kasal (right) talks with fellow Marines about leadership after a presentation at Camp Pendleton.

Marines patrol the streets of Haqlaniyah, Iraq, in a LAV-25 armored personnel carrier.

Marines have bravely defended the United States throughout the country's history. Time and again, they have risked their lives—never thinking twice about putting themselves in harm's way. Their tales show us more than just the strength of our fighting men and women. They display the incredible depth of human courage in the line of fire.

battalion (buh-TAL-yuhn)—a large group of soldiers

bayonet (BAY-uh-net)—a long metal blade attached to the end of a musket or rifle

convoy (KON-voi)—a group of vehicles traveling together, usually accompanied by armed forces

disband (dis-BAND)—to remove a military unit from active service

insurgent (in-SUR-junt)—a person who rebels and fights against his or her country's ruling government and those supporting it

mortar (MOR-tur)—a short cannon that fires shells or rockets high in the air

motto (MOT-oh)—a short statement that tells what a person or organization believes in or stands for

Nazi (NOT-see)—a member of a political party led by Adolf Hitler; the Nazis ruled Germany from 1933 to 1945

platoon (pluh-TOON)—a small group of soldiers who work together

posthumous (POHST-huh-muhss)—coming or happening after death

private (PRYE-vit)—a soldier of the lowest rank

shrapnel (SHRAP-nuhl)—pieces that have broken off something after an explosion

surrender (suh-REN-dur)—to give up or admit defeat in battle

terrorist (TER-ur-ist)—a person who uses violence to kill, injure, or make people and governments afraid

trench (TRENCH)—a long, deep area dug into the ground with dirt piled up on one side for defense

READ MORE

Huey, Lois Miner. *Voices of World War II: Stories from the Front Lines.* Voices of War. Mankato, Minn.: Capstone, 2011.

Hunter, Nick. *Military Survival.* Extreme Survival. Chicago: Raintree, 2011.

Person, Stephen. *Navy SEAL Team Six in Action.* Special Ops II. New York: Bearport, 2014.

Williams, Brian. *Sailors Under Fire.* War Stories. Chicago: Heinemann, 2012.

SELECT BIBLIOGRAPHY

Baines, Christofer P. "Marine Receives Navy Cross for Actions in Vietnam War." U.S. Department of Defense, www.defense.gov/News/NewsArticle.aspx?ID=62788.

Cordero, Jeffrey. "Decades Later, Marine Awarded for Heroism in Vietnam." 9th Marine Corps District, www.9thmcd.marines.mil/News/NewsArticleDisplay/tabid/4722/Article/142522/decades-later-marine-awarded-for-heroism-in-vietnam.aspx.

Frank, Benis. "Colonel Peter Julien Ortiz: OSS Marine, Actor, Californian." California State Military Museum, www.militarymuseum.org/Ortiz.html.

Fuentes, Gidget. "3/5 Sergeant to be Awarded Silver Star." Marine Corps Times, March 23, 2012, www.marinecorpstimes.com/article/20120323/NEWS/203230318/3-5-sergeant-awarded-Silver-Star.

Mortensen, Mark. *George W. Hamilton, USMC: America's Greatest World War I Hero.* Jefferson, N.C.: McFarland & Company, 2011.

Proser, Jim, and Jerry Cutter. *I'm Staying with My Boys: The Heroic Life of Sgt. John Basilone, USMC.* New York: St. Martin's Griffin, 2010.

Yang, Eleanor. "War Hero: You Don't Just Sit Idly and Watch." The Morning Call, January 14, 2001, http://articles.mcall.com/2001-01-14/news/3349660_1_iraqi-brigade-desert-storm-war-hero.

FactHound offers a safe, fun way to find Internet sites related to this book. All of the sites on FactHound have been researched by our staff.

Here's all you do:

Visit www.facthound.com

Type in this code: 9781476599359

 Check out projects, games and lots more at www.capstonekids.com